EVERY CHILD DESERVES...

By Zaden and his two Dads

with Illustrations by Jonathan Thunder

For - Zaden

To – All youth in foster care and LGBTQ families that love them

Every Child Deserves…

Printed in the United States of America

First Printing, 2017

ISBN - 978-1-5323-4282-0

First Edition First Printing

@ 2017 Philip McAdoo

Published 2017

Self-published

www.philipmcadoo.com

There are thousands of children who are touched by foster care.

Thousands of children whose lives never get fully lived.

But...

Every child deserves...

to catch a fish in an open stream...

hot chocolate on a cold night...

to score
the
winning goal...

to catch a flyball...

and kisses...

to swim to the
edge of the
ocean . . .

and sleep under

the stars...

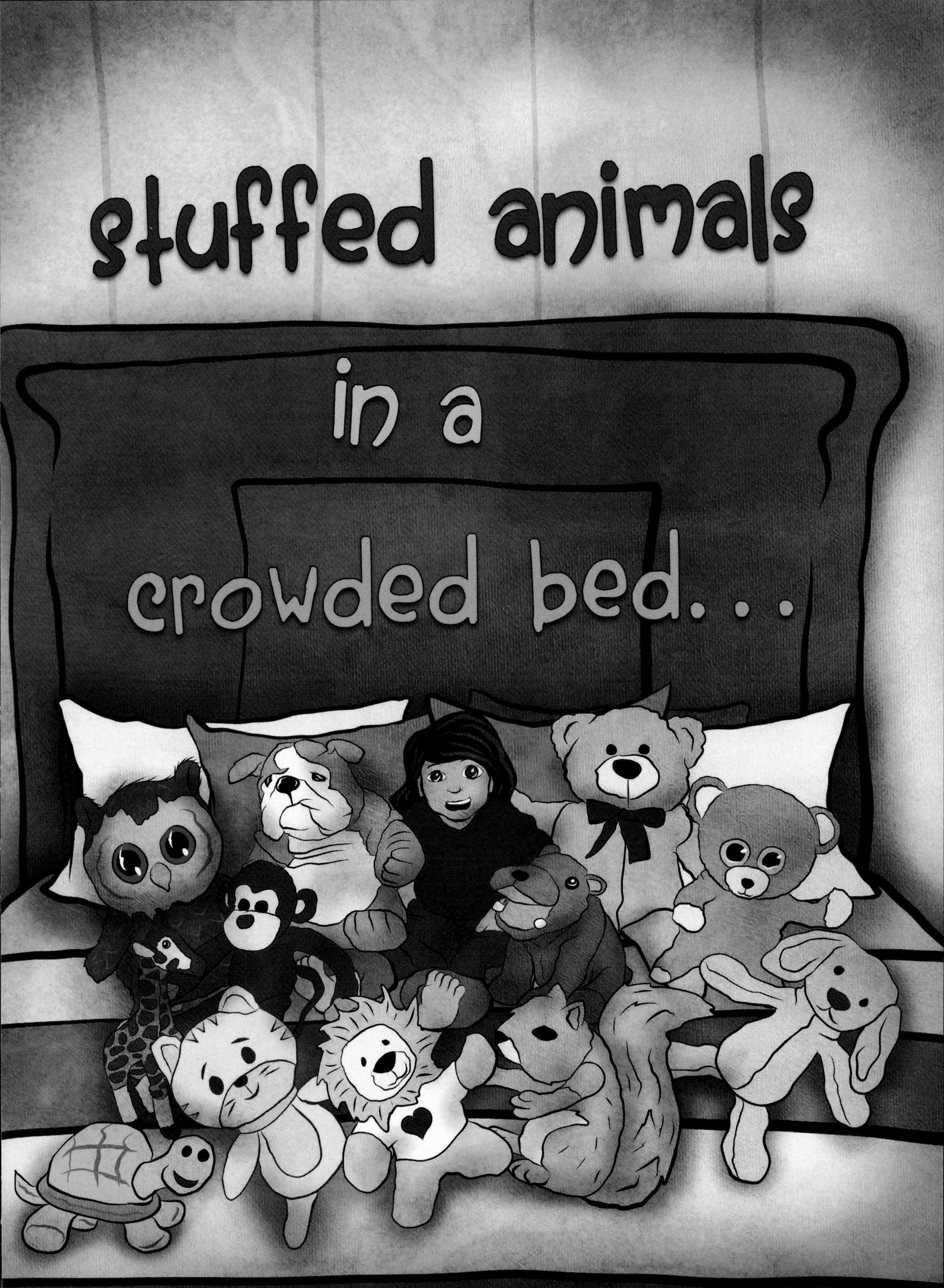
stuffed animals
in a
crowded bed...

dreams...

and the wisdom of GRANDPARENTS...

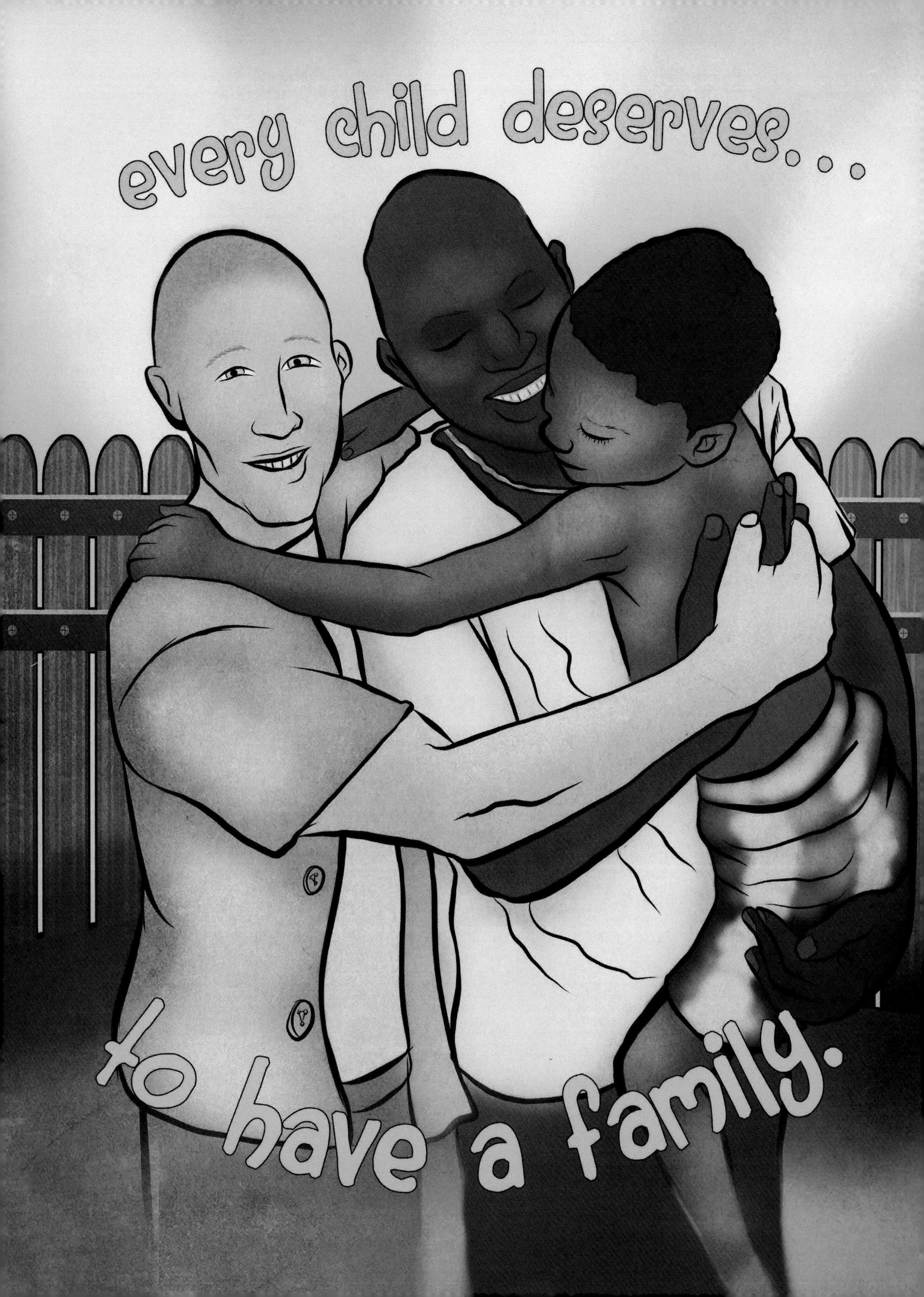
every child deserves...
to have a family.

Philip McAdoo

Dr. Philip McAdoo: Broadway productions of The Lion King and Rent, appeared in readings of The Book of Mormon and Wicked, and worked in television and film. He is a graduate of the University of North Carolina at Chapel Hill with a degree in communications studies, holds an MA in transformative leadership from The California Institute of Integral Studies, and earned a doctorate of education from The University of Pennsylvania in the Graduate School of Education.

As an LGBTQ activist, Dr. McAdoo was invited to join politician and civil rights activist Rep. John Lewis speaking in support of the Every Child Deserves a Family Act to introduce legislation to Congress that would lower some of the barriers faced by same-sex couples who want to adopt children from foster care. Dr. McAdoo and his family have been featured in The Huffington Post, ABC News, and on the cover of magazines and articles advocating for the rights of LGBTQ individuals and families.

Philip currently is the Director of Equity, Justice and Community at the Sidwell Friends School in Washington, DC.

Zaden

Zaden aka "Z man" is fun, smart, defiant, smelly, sweaty, cautious, curious, mischievous, smooth, silly, love, joy, light and HOPE.

About the Illustrator

Jonathan R Thunder is a painter, illustrator, film maker and digital media artist currently residing in Duluth, Mn. His work has been featured in many state, regional, and national exhibitions, as well as in local and international publications. Thunder has won several first place awards in swaia's annual class 'x' moving images competition for animation and experimental film. Thunder is a tribal member of the Red Lake Band of Ojibwe.